How To
Be A Reasonably
THIN
Teenage Girl

To Judy,
My "firefly" CWC friend.
Good Luck and keep
writing. Bonnie Luber

How To
Be A Reasonably
THIN
Teenage Girl

Without Starving, Losing Your Friends
or Running Away from Home

by BONNIE L. LUKES

with illustrations by Carol Nicklaus

Atheneum · New York

Atheneum
Macmillan Publishing Company
866 Third Avenue, New York, NY 10022
Collier Macmillan Canada, Inc.

Composition by Heritage Printers, Charlotte, North Carolina
Printed and bound by Fairfield Graphics, Fairfield, Pennsylvania
Designed by Mary Ahern

10 9 8 7 6 5 4 3

Library of Congress Cataloging in Publication Data

Lukes, Bonnie L.
How to be a reasonably thin teenage girl.

SUMMARY: Suggestions for taking weight off and keeping
it off through modifying attitudes, eating nutritiously,
and exercising.
1. Adolescent girls—Nutrition—Juvenile literature.
2. Reducing—Juvenile literature.   [1. Weight control.
2. Nutrition.   3. Adolescent girls—Nutrition]
I. Title
RJ144.L85   1986   613.2'5   86-3347
ISBN 0-689-31269-5

To

my husband,

JOHN,

who made it all

possible.

Contents

How To
Be A Reasonably
THIN
Teenage Girl

1

First the bad news

So, you're a blimp. So you had to lie on the floor this morning to zip your jeans. And you say you missed the big game because your oversized shirt (the one you try to convince yourself covers everything) was in the laundry?

Maybe you should go on a diet.

"No kidding?," you snarl, "I've only been on twelve this year—one for each month—and all I got was fatter. It's no use. I just can't lose."

Yes, you can. Would an ex-fatty lie to you? But first, we've got to adjust your attitude.

For instance

Think back on those five hundred other diet books you've read. Remember how along about the second page you could always count on the author to make a statement like: "On this diet you can eat all you want. You'll never be hungry." Then, a hundred pages later, the little bombshell is dropped that "all you want" certainly doesn't include pizza and chocolate cake.

How to be a reasonably thin teenage girl

This is often followed by the funniest line ever written: "You *must* eat *all* the food allowed on this diet." As though we wouldn't!

You won't find that kind of rubbish in this book. So, before we go on, let's make sure we understand each other.

First, *you can't eat everything you want and lose weight.* Second, *you will be hungry.*

Oh, not hungry like fainting, empty-stomach hungry. But, hungry like "I'd kill for a hot fudge sundae."

Well, what'd you expect? Like the man said, there ain't no free lunch. Every potato chip counts. But trust me, you can learn to handle this craziness.

2

How'd you get so fat anyway?

It's your mother's fault, right? It's your mother's and your father's fault. They're overweight and you inherited it. It's the schools. They put too much pressure on you. Or . . . you're just unlucky. It's not that you eat a lot, it's that everything you eat turns to fat. Maybe, but I doubt it.

The scientific fellas say that a tendency to get fat may be inherited, but all the facts aren't in yet. And even if it proves to be true, so what?

The plain truth is that your body doesn't need as much food as you've been feeding it, and the excess has become fat.

I like to eat—don't you?

The psych set has done a lot of research on why we overeat. They talk about boredom, depression, guilt and anxiety. Fun things like that. Those are all good reasons, but personally I overate because I liked to eat. I still like to eat. I just know how to handle it now.

5

How to be a reasonably thin teenage girl

If I felt sad, I ate to make myself feel better. On the other hand, if something super-fantastic happened, I ate to celebrate.

There didn't seem to be any emotional or physical state that would keep me from eating, outside of the stomach flu, and I didn't get that often enough to help.

Other people caught a cold and lost five pounds—I gained five. Other girls lost their boyfriends and dropped ten pounds along with him. Me, I gained ten the first week he was gone.

If you want to analyze why you overeat, go ahead. It might help. But I'll just bet that like me—any old excuse will do. It's raining. It's not raining. I don't feel well. I feel terrific. I've got a date. I don't have a date. And on and on and on.

3

How fat are you?

We won't waste time with weight charts since they don't mean much, and you probably know them by heart anyway. I'd like to say it's how you feel when you look in a mirror that counts, but that's dangerous. The current craze for thinness can sometimes make a ninety-pounder look in the mirror and see a fat person.

A better and safer way is to use this simple, old rule: Allow 100 pounds for a height of five feet, and add five pounds for each inch over five feet. That's reasonably thin.

But wait a minute

Let's face hard, cold facts. Say you're 5'4" and weigh 150 pounds. According to our rule, you should weigh 120 (according to the fashion mags—85). Of course, 85 is ridiculous, but 120 *for you, at this time,* may be just as farfetched.

Why not set your goal for 130? At 130, you won't be asked to stand in for a model, but no one's going to turn and yell, "Hey, Fatso," either.

How to be a reasonably thin teenage girl

Once you prove you can keep your weight at 130, maybe you'll try for 120. Maybe. Or, you may see how nice you can look at 130—particularly by choosing clothes carefully—and decide you'd rather be not quite so thin and able to indulge in a chocolate shake once in a while.

It's a matter of deciding what you can live with. DON'T THINK ONLY OF GETTING TO A CERTAIN WEIGHT. THINK ABOUT WHETHER YOU CAN STAY AT THAT WEIGHT.

Anyone can lose weight—very few can keep it off. Those who succeed have learned to be realistic. They know, for example, that it's smarter to stay at 130 (which is certainly a heck of a lot better than 150) than it is to force their weight down to 120, then go back up to 150 and beyond, back down again, back up again and once more around the track.

At 130, you can stand in front of a mirror and say, "Hey, I don't look like a movie star, but by golly, I do look good." And let's face it, the odds are that no matter how much weight you lose, or what kind of eyeshadow you buy, you probably won't look like a movie star anyway.

Daydreaming is fine for relaxation, but you have to live in the real world.

4

How fast will I lose?

You'll lose about a pound a week, although you'll drop more the first week because of water loss.

No, it will *not* take you forever to lose the weight. Actually, if you're twenty pounds overweight, it'll take twenty weeks or five months. If you're thirty pounds over, it'll take—well, you figure it out.

Sure, you can lose faster. You can lose five pounds in two days. Haven't you done it a hundred times? The Atkins, Stillman, Bronx, Beverly Hills, Pickle and Potato diet, Twinkie and Tangerine diet. You tried them all and knocked off five pounds like nothing, right? Sure you did. And you gained it right back plus more, didn't you?

As a matter of fact, you probably went on one glorious binge after each diet ended, and then cried yourself to sleep. Don't try to con an ex-fatty. I tried 'em all. And every one of them worked. For a while.

Washing an elephant

How do you wash something as big as an elephant? You wash a section at a time, and before you know it the whole elephant is squeaky clean.

You use the same strategy to lose your fat. Break your weight into five-pound goals. If you think in terms of twenty-five, fifty or 100 pounds, you'll sink into a black depression and go searching for some gooey treat to make yourself feel better.

Another way to head off depression and defeat at the scale is to WEIGH ONLY ONCE A WEEK, always on the same day, and preferably first thing in the morning immediately after going to the bathroom.

How fast will I lose?

There are two reasons for this rule. First, your weight bounces back and forth some because of fluid balance or imbalance, and second if you weigh every day you expect to see a pound gone every time you step on the scale. The time for daily weighing is after you get the weight off. *And you will get it off.*

5

Check it out

Let's say you weigh 150 pounds, and you're 5'2" tall. Using our rule, you should weigh 110 pounds. But you're going to forget that and set your sights on 125. That's your long-range goal. Your immediate goal will be 145.

When the scale reads 145, your immediate goal will change to 140 and on down the line. But once you reach 125, you'll quit trying to lose and concentrate on staying at that weight.

I didn't say you'd stop counting calories. You'll continue to count—eating the amount needed to maintain 125 pounds (see the chart at the end of this chapter). After you stay at 125 for a month—within a pound or two and with no wild fluctuations—then you can decide whether to remain there or move on down.

Make your decision according to how difficult it is for you to hold at 125. If it's a real struggle, there's no point in going lower—at least not at this time.

After you get used to eating less and become accustomed to wearing a smaller size (and all the fun that goes with that), you may just find that one day you'll be ready to start down

Check it out

again. Be that as it may, you can take tremendous pride in the fact that you've lost twenty-five pounds forever.

How many calories to lose
this whopping pound a week?

Don't be sarcastic. A pound a week is more than you've been losing, and it's going to stay off. Meanwhile, back to our 150-pound dieter. Let's give her a name. We'll call her Mary. To figure how many calories Mary's eating daily in order to keep her weight at 150 pounds, you do this:

$$
\begin{array}{r}
150 \\
\times \quad 15 \\
\hline
2{,}250
\end{array}
$$

Mary's eating around 2,250 calories a day to maintain her 150 pounds. You can figure yours the same way—your weight times 15.

Now to lose weight, Mary must do this:

$$
\begin{array}{l}
2{,}250 \text{ (amount Mary's now eating)} \\
- \quad 500 \\
\hline
1{,}750 \text{ (amount Mary must eat to lose a pound a week)}
\end{array}
$$

After each five-pound loss, Mary will adjust this figure, decreasing the amount by 75 calories as shown in the chart on the following page.

How to be a reasonably thin teenage girl

WEIGHT	NUMBER OF CALS NEEDED TO MAINTAIN THIS WEIGHT	NUMBER OF CALS NEEDED TO LOSE WEIGHT
150	2,250	1,750
145	2,175	1,675
140	2,100	1,600
135	2,025	1,525
130	1,950	1,450
125	1,875	1,375
120	1,800	1,300
115	1,725	1,225
110	1,650	1,150

6

The reward

If you have a severe pain in your back, and for all you know, it will never go away, the pain will seem unbearable.

But if you know that after resting a day or two the pain will disappear, it's much easier to bear.

Most anything can be tolerated as long as relief is somewhere in sight. What I've discovered in dieting is that it'd better not be too far away.

Diet specialists, psychologists and all those other skinny experts always advise rewarding yourself with something besides food—a new blouse, a bracelet, a movie—something you enjoy.

It's not that it's bad advice, but it won't work right away, and in the diet game, the most important time is IN THE MEANTIME. So until you learn to reward yourself in other ways, let me tell you what worked for me.

My favorite food is ice cream. So naturally, ice cream was (and is) my reward. All week long (and some of them can get awfully long when you're dieting), it was easier to pass up the gravy or the butter or the second helpings by reminding myself that on Saturday I could have my ice cream.

Why Saturday? Because that was my weigh-in day. If I had a temporary gain from the ice cream, it would be long gone by the next Saturday weigh-in.

First, *understand this*. I didn't have a banana split, a hot fudge sundae or any other such gooey concoction. This is a reward, not a food orgy. But I did order two scoops of whatever kind of ice cream I wanted.

I usually brought the ice cream home to eat and either took it to my room or to the backyard—anyplace I could be alone. I didn't read or watch T.V. I simply experienced that ice cream in every possible sense—the smell, the texture, the overall taste.

16

The reward

Of course, you'll handle this in your own way. Perhaps you'd rather be with friends when you enjoy your reward. Perhaps you prefer french fries to ice cream. That's up to you.

But remember: this is not a pig-out. This is a reward within reason. ONE FAVORITE FOOD IN A REASONABLE AMOUNT.

Now many times—O.K., O.K., every time—after I finish the last bite of ice cream, I wish I could have another scoop. What I do is remind myself that there'll be another reward next week (if I don't mess this one up) and I get up and leave the place.

And that's the reason you'll either go out for your reward, or bring home the *exact amount* you figure you should eat. That way, you can't have more, the craving will vanish in a few minutes, and you can begin looking forward to next week.

We chubs must keep explaining to ourselves that food will be available at the next meal, or the next day or the next week. So much of the time, we act as though this piece of candy or this slice of pizza is the last one left on earth.

The best thing about this reward is that you can really enjoy it. You don't have the guilts. You're not messing up. You *planned* this treat.

This weekly reward not only helped me toe the line during my diet, but it helped me hold the line afterwards. When I reached my goal, I didn't run out and buy a gallon of chocolate chocolate chip ice cream to celebrate as I'd done so many times before.

I wasn't starved for ice cream because I'd been enjoying it right along. I also learned by the time I reached goal that I didn't need to eat a gallon of ice cream at one sitting—a dish of ice cream is enjoyable also.

I should point out that on this Reward Day, I ate my usual diet meals. In other words, I still counted calories that day. If, say, my calorie allowance was 1,800 cals per day that week, that's how many I ate. The ice cream was in addition to those 1,800 cals and naturally put me over my limit. But as long as I followed the diet faithfully throughout the rest of the week, I still lost my pound by the next Saturday weigh-in.

Remember to kiss
(keep it simple, Snoopy)

The simpler you keep your diet, the better. Start fooling around with so-called low-calorie sauces and desserts, and you're in trouble.

You may find a recipe for chocolate pudding that's only 75 cals for a half-cup. If we chubs could eat one half-cup of anything, especially a dessert, we wouldn't be in the shape we're in. We like to finish things, and if the recipe is for four servings, that's 300 cals.

If you're that crazy for pudding, make it your reward for the week, and go out to a restaurant for it. Or make it yourself. Just be sure your family is home at the time to finish it off then and there. You don't want leftover pudding lurking in the fridge screaming your name.

7

The big four/calorie-counting diet

Don't expect me to make up a month's supply of diet menus for you. Having someone else plan your menus doesn't work. I don't know how your mother cooks or what you like or what you hate. Only you know that. Your diet must be made up of foods you don't gag on, or you'll never stick with it.

Anyway, it's no big deal. First, you calculate how many calories you're allowed (see Chapter 6). Second, look in Appendix B for the Basic 4 food listings. Now, choose (totaling the calories as you go) two foods from the Meat Group, three from the Milk, four from the Fruits and Veggies and four from the Bread and Cereal Group. If you have cals left over, splurge on whatever.

Once you get this 2-3-4-4 formula in your head, there's one more thing to learn. It's called JUGGLING. Learn it well because you'll use it the rest of your life. Like most things, the best way to learn is to practice, practice, practice until it's something you do without thinking.

How to be a reasonably thin teenage girl

Take the Fruit and Veggie Group as an example. If you choose a starchy veggie for dinner—a potato maybe—then you won't also choose corn or peas because you'll soon learn that will shoot the calorie count up too high. You'll pick green beans or broccoli—one of the lower cal veggies.

It's the same with all the groups. Juggle, balance, exchange until you come up with meals that satisfy you. Make it a game. But remember some days will be more fun than others. Some days, no matter how much you juggle, you'll still be dying for a piece of fudge or a bowl of mashed potatoes smothered in gravy. Those days you bite the bullet, or if you can't find a bullet, use a celery stick. And always remember Reward Day.

To give you an idea of how to plan your menus, I'm including a sample one-day menu. So, with the understanding that this menu will need modifying to suit you, here's one day in my diet when I was eating 1,300 cals a day.

BREAKFAST

1 oz. cereal with sweetner	110
1 cup low-fat milk*	140
4 oz. orange juice**	60
	310 TOTAL

Another thing about this breakfast. I ate, and still eat, cereal because I like it. I could have had an egg and toast and

---

* Although I drink only nonfat milk and have learned to like it (it does take getting used to), I can't stand it on cereal. Maybe you can. If so, you'll save sixty extra cals right there for something else.

** One of your four choices from the Fruit and Veggie Group should be a good source of Vitamin C. Strawberries, grapefruit, oranges, tomatoes and cantaloupe are all loaded with Vitamin C but not with calories.

juice. Whatever satisfies you. Hold it! We're not talking waffles and a quart of maple syrup. Still, if you're really into waffles, you could have:

1 *frozen Jumbo Aunt Jemina Waffle**	90
1 *tsp. diet margarine*	30
4 *tbs. lite syrup***	120
½ *cup orange juice*	60
	300 TOTAL CALORIES

---

* We go frozen because nobody is going to mix batter for one waffle.

** You can see what I like, but how about you? Maybe you'd prefer more diet margarine and less syrup. Just another example of why you must plan your own-menus.

How to be a reasonably thin teenage girl

MIDMORNING SNACK*

Apple, peach or two plums, small banana (remember there's no law that says you can't cut a banana in half), or have whatever fruit is in season—one serving, that is. For this particular calorie allotment (1,300), I kept the morning and afternoon snack to no more than 100 cals.

LUNCH

| *Tuna Sandwich* | 250 cals | (3 oz. water-packed tuna mixed with two tbs. of low-cal mayo, minced onion or celery, or both, and a thick slice of tomato on two slices of whole wheat bread) |

| *8 oz. Non-fat Milk* | 80 cals |

330 TOTAL

AFTERNOON SNACK**

½ cantaloupe and two vanilla wafers   100 cals TOTAL

NOTE: If cantaloupe isn't in season, or you despise it, you could have an orange. Or maybe you can't handle vanilla wafers and wouldn't stop with two, or even if you did, would hear them calling you from the pantry all the rest of the afternoon. In

---

* If you don't need a midmorning snack, save the calories for later when you're really craving something. Personally, I begin fretting if I think I can't eat anything until lunch. You may prefer using the snack cals as part of breakfast or lunch. Whatever.

** Same rules as for morning snack.

that case, forget the wafers. Instead of the canta-
loupe-wafer combo, you could have any one of
the following combinations for 100 calories.
One slice diet cheese plus two saltines
One serving of fresh fruit
Two breadsticks and a diet soda
One cup low-cal Ovaltine, and either one slice of diet
  cheese or two saltines
One fruit-flavored popsicle (3 oz.)
One Dreamsicle (2½ oz.)
One box raisins (1 oz.)
One slice whole wheat bread with two tsps. low-sugar jelly
Four cups popcorn popped without oil, no butter added

You can see the possibilities are endless, but only you
know what will tide you over until dinner with the least
amount of self-pity.

DINNER

One split chicken breast (3 oz.)	150
fried in non-stick skillet with skin	
removed	
Broccoli (average serving)	50
no butter or margarine added	
Small baked potato with one	
tbs. diet margarine	100
Green salad with low-cal dressing	100
Breadstick	50
	450 TOTAL

About after-dinner snacks. If you can possibly form the
habit of not eating after dinner, do it. It'll not only help you

lose, but it'll help you maintain your weight once you reach goal.

It's so easy to start off with a small snack, be lulled into a hypnotic trance by the T.V., and come out of it to find yourself finishing off a pint of chocolate chocolate chip. It's discouraging to have this happen after you've made it through an entire day. It's like losing the game in the last half of the ninth.

If you must have something, have a liquid such as low-cal soda, low-cal hot chocolate or a cup of nonfat milk—something that doesn't need chewing. Chewing triggers all kinds of food fantasies and sets the salivary glands in motion.

8

A word of explanation

If you total the calories consumed on my sample diet day, you'll find that they add up to 1305. Close enough.

Now, notice how I covered the Basic 4. Milk at breakfast (on the cereal) and a glass with dinner satisfied my milk needs. Since teenagers need three to four servings a day, you'll need to work in another glass. That's why nonfat milk is a good choice if you must have an after-dinner snack.

Meanwhile, back at the sample diet day. The tuna at lunch and the chicken at dinner fulfilled the meat requirement.

As for the fruit and veggie group, I went beyond what was needed. The orange juice, cantaloupe, broccoli and the fruit for the morning snack would have sufficed, but I also had a potato at dinner:

Unfortunately . . .

The trouble is, most families don't eat like that. You're much more apt to come to the table and find lasagne, a tossed green salad with blue cheese dressing, garlic bread dripping with butter and chocolate cake with chocolate frosting.

How to be a reasonably thin teenage girl

Now what do you do? Sit and nibble on a salad without dressing and glower around at the rest of the family—the creeps—pigging out on lasagne, feeling sorrier and sorrier for yourself, working up to a binge of Hershey bars in a dark corner of your room later?

No. You don't do that.

First, you silently remind yourself how really sick and tired you are of being fat. Take just a minute to remember the last time you tried to zip your jeans. Worse than that, remember what you looked like once you were stuffed into them.

Second, you buckle on your willpower and say no thank you to the garlic bread. Sweetly, you say that—not snarling that you're on a diet and any idiot should know you can't have bread. (Actually, it's not that you can't have bread, you just can't afford bread and lasagne at the same time.)

Third, you excuse yourself from the table, and get your low-calorie dressing from the refrigerator and your breadstick from the freezer. (They'll be there, because you'll have seen to that before you started your diet.) Pour yourself a glass of skim milk and return to the table. Place a generous square of lasagne on your plate. (In foods like lasagne, you're knocking off two of the Basic 4 requirements in one shot. See Appendix B for further explanation.)

Now, you have no reason to feel sorry for yourself. Eat slowly so when the others are reaching for seconds, you'll have food left.

When it's dessert time, ask to be excused, and be cheerful about it so the family doesn't press you to have "just a little"—something that you and I know is impossible.

If chocolate cake is your favorite dessert, save a piece for your Reward Day. If it isn't, but you still like it a lot and would love to have some, remind yourself that passing it up doesn't mean you'll never have another chance at it. Honest. There'll

A word of explanation

be another chocolate cake baked someday. It's not on the endangered species list.

Maybe you have the kind of mother who'll prepare that special plate for you every night, separate from what the rest of the family eats. That makes her a real sweetheart, and we know it means you'll be able to count on her support in things like keeping low-cal foods in stock. But I don't think it's wise for her to make a special meal for you each night. The reason being that you live in a spaghetti-cream-sauced-french-fried world, and you'd better get on with learning how to handle it.

9

What if I mess up?

"What if" should not be the question. Make it "When I." Because you *will* mess up. There'll come a day when the crazies will take over.

"I don't care," you'll shriek, tearing into a box of butter crunch cookies. Any number of things can bring this about. A broken romance, a fight with your parents, premenstrual tension, final exams looming ominously on the horizon, or maybe just a crazed desire for butter crunch cookies.

After the ball

O.K. You've done it. The box is empty. You're stuffed and you feel like a loser (the wrong kind). There are things to do at this point and things not to do.

You *don't* say, "Oh, well, I've already blown it anyway," and run to the refrigerator for some salami to take the sweet taste out of your mouth.

You *do* say, "All right. I'm human and I blew it." Forgive yourself and get on with it.

How to be a reasonably thin teenage girl

You *don't* skip dinner to make up for an afternoon binge or breakfast if it was a nighttime splurge.

You *do* follow your diet exactly as before the slip-up. If this crazies attack happens the day before your weighing day—skip weighing that week.

Until I learned to let my goofs go and get right back on the diet, I never consistently lost weight because everytime I messed up, I'd give up and head for the ice cream shop. It's like that old story of falling off a horse, you've got to climb right back on and the sooner the better.

10

What about my social life?

O.K. fine, you say. All that stuff's all right for everyday, but aren't there any special occasions? Must I live the rest of my life in a cave without ever tasting another pizza? Certainly not. Caves are dull and damp.

Let's say it's the Friday night football game, and afterwards the gang's meeting at Louie's for pizza. What are you going to do? Bring along a head of lettuce? Don't be silly. You'd never get it in your purse.

Here, in two of the most important words in a dieter's vocabulary, is what you're going to do. PLAN AHEAD.

Example. For breakfast on the day of the big game, you'll have a hard-boiled egg and one slice of toast that you've ever so lightly skimmed with diet margarine (160 cals total). Mid-morning, you'll munch an apple (80 cals). Come lunchtime, you'll have a can of water-packed tuna with nothing mixed in, a breadstick and a diet drink. You have now had 480 cals. Naturally, you may choose different foods as long as you keep the total around 500.

If you can handle it, don't have anything after school. Sometimes, it's easier to make it through an afternoon feeling hungry when you're looking forward to a fun evening. But, if you can't hang on, have a couple of cups of unbuttered popcorn.

Because I did it myself for so many years, I know exactly what you're thinking. You're saying to yourself, "Well, if I can only have 500 cals until dinner, I might just as well have a couple of glazed doughnuts for breakfast and be done with it. Don't do it. A little protein, a little starch, a little natural sugar from the apple, these will get you through the day. Refined sugar won't. You'll feel good for a few minutes, then POW.

You've made it to game time. You're seated in the bleachers. The referee blows his whistle. The worst part's over. Right? Wrong.

Here they come (and so many of them are skinny, that's what drives you crazy) carrying their hot dogs, their popcorn, their candy bars. Maybe you could have just one . . . . Don't do it. Have a diet soda. Put your thoughts on the captain of the debating team sitting in front of you or on the quarterback down on the field, and you'll forget about food. O.K., O.K., you won't forget it completely. We never forget it completely. We just learn to tune it out for longer periods of time.

From the tables down at Louie's

By golly you made it. Here you are at the pizza parlor. What's that? You say the smell of the food is making you feel faint. COME ON.

The waiter brings the fresh, steaming pizza to your table. Now what? Here's what. You'll have two slices—one if it's the deep-dish, thick-crust kind. Eat slowly. Savor each and every bite. Use your mouth for something besides eating. Make brilliant, witty conversation. Smile a lot (you can't do that with your mouth full).

What about my social life?

Make your portion last until the last piece of pizza has been eaten. Don't make a big deal of how much you're not eating. If you don't mention it, nobody will notice. Don't set yourself up so you're "forced" to eat more.

Nutritionally speaking, this hasn't been an ideal day. You didn't cover all of the Basic 4, but one day does not an eating pattern make. Just don't have too many of these days in a row.

Before we leave the pizza day, I must remind you that to make a diet work, you have to make it your diet. The above description is the way I would have handled that particular day. It may work better for you to eat your normal day's number of calories and just have a diet soda when the others are eating pizza. Perhaps you'd rather have had a hot dog and soda during the game instead of pizza later.

You have to try different ways of handling situations until you find what works for you. Either way you go, it won't be easy. But out of several different ways, *one will be easier for you than the others.* That's what you're looking for.

But what will I do at the slumber party?

So, you're invited to a slumber party. What will happen at that party besides laughing and teasing and talking about boys? I know. You know. FOOD is going to happen. It'll be all over the place and not a carrot stick in sight. Just cookies and candies and chips. How can you resist those goodies all night long. What on earth will you do?

I say *go for it.*

Yes, go for it. For a couple of reasons. One is that even if you last the night without overeating, you're apt to feel so deprived and sorry for yourself that you'll make up for it the entire next week or even month. (This is the voice of experience speaking.)

The second reason is that it's better to make the decision to go off the diet before you go to the party. If you *plan* to go off your diet, you eliminate the guilt you suffer when you *fall off* your diet.

After all, if you plan to eat, you're just following through on what you said you'd do. If you go determined not to eat and you do—then you've failed—and it's apt to send you into a tailspin.

But watch out! If the party is on Saturday, don't start eating in anticipation on Friday. Follow your diet right up until the time you walk into the party.

The danger in pulling out all the stops is that you get the taste of all that "good stuff" you haven't tasted for a while. So get a firm grip on yourself the next day, because you must GET RIGHT BACK ON YOUR DIET. By getting back in the routine quickly, you may not lose your pound that week, but you'll not gain either.

If the day after the party is your weighing day, DON'T WEIGH. Wait another week. And don't weigh just out of curiosity to see how much damage you did. All that does is set you up for depression, which leads to self-pity, which leads to saying, "What's the use?," which leads to being fat for the rest of your life.

Then, too, there's the possibility of weighing and finding you stayed the same. That's a danger because it will encourage wishful thinking. Why, look, you'll say, I didn't gain a bit and then you'll go on eating that day, and the next, and the day after that . . . . Trust me. Don't weigh.

Also, let's use a little common sense. If the day after the party would ordinarily be your Reward Day—forget it, Love. You've had your reward.

One other thing. You can't go to a party where you're going to go crazy on food every other night, or even every other

What about my social life?

week. You cannot eat your cake and have it too—at least, not very often—because it tends to settle around the hips. Pass up some parties until you've lost more weight and gained more control. It'll be worth it.

11

Danger
time

There's something about coming home from somewhere, anywhere, that makes us chubs think we should eat. I can leave the house at 9:00 A.M., come back at 10:00 A.M., and because I've been out, I think I should have food the minute I enter the door. That's when an Emergency Box can be a diet saver.

What's an Emergency Box? Well, it's a box you use in an emergency. It doesn't have to be a box, just some kind of container, and it should belong to you. You can see to that by taping your name on it along with some pointed remarks about the danger of bodily harm to anyone found tampering with said box.

Store the E-Box in the refrigerator. In it, place low-cal cheese slices, some hard-boiled eggs, carrot sticks, celery sticks, cold cooked broccoli, green peppers, cherry tomatoes, dill pickles (watch these—lots of salt)—any low-cal foods you like (you don't have to love them).

Now when you come home from school half-starved, or you think you are, grab from the E-Box instead of the cookie jar.

Double danger

About that coming home from school. Be on guard because it can be a tough time of day. Chances are good that you'll be the only one home and there you are, just you and the goodies, with no one to see, and if no one sees you eat, the calories won't count, right? WRONG.

How to be a reasonably thin teenage girl

You should prepare for this by having a snack already prepared. But in case you goofed on that, have something from the E-Box while you fix a snack. At the very least, have the snack planned in your mind before you reach home. Otherwise, you're apt to go through the pantry and fridge grabbing this and that and everything else.

The difficulty is, that prepared snack or not, you may not want to stop eating if all you have to look forward to is a ton of homework and cleaning the bathroom for your mother.

You have several choices. Either do part of the work first and then have your snack (that works best for me), or plan something pleasant for yourself following the snack before you hit the books or chores.

You can also plan a reward (not food) for yourself after you've finished the chores. You have to find what works for you. But if you plan a nonfood reward, it must be something you truly enjoy whether it's reading a mushy love story, talking on the phone, scratching the cat's tummy, or here's my favorite: Cut Sue Ann Smirkel's picture out of the yearbook, and use it for a dart board. You remember Sue Ann—cheerleader, homecoming queen, the lead in the school play, weighs 64 pounds, eats one lettuce leaf and simpers, "Oh my, I'm simply stuffed." Right. I knew you'd recognize her.

12

It's called exercise, or get off your duff and do something

It's basic. The more you move, the more calories you burn. Or . . . the more exercise you get, the more you can eat. Or . . . if you eat less and exercise more, you'll lose faster than if you just eat less. And . . . exercising guarantees that the weight you lose is actually FAT, not lean muscle.

Mention exercise and after the moans and groans die down, the Fatty Chubs Chorus begins.

First Verse: There's no point in exercising. "Why it takes one hour of walking to burn up 210 calories," they say with a snicker. O.K. So it does. Speed up and you'll burn 300 cals. And you don't need to walk an hour. Even if you walk only fifteen minutes a day, in four days that'll add up to one hour and 250 to 300 cals burned. No matter how you look at it, you're ahead.

Second Verse: "If I exercise, it'll just make me hungrier. I'll eat twice as much."

It's called exercise . . .

That's true if you're trim and lean and in good condition. But then you're not, or you wouldn't be reading this book.

Fat people respond differently to exercise—they do *not* experience increased appetite unless they exercise excessively. Lab experiments have proved this. Fat animals, which were exercised one hour a day, ate a smaller amount of food than those exercised *less* than an hour a day or not at all!

Meanwhile, outside the lab

So much for statistics. A couple of years ago, I started running every morning—no marathons—just a moderate run around the park. The first week I went home and ate a bigger breakfast than usual. Not because I was hungrier, but because that old enemy, Wishful Thinking, whispered, "Oh, my dear, you've had all that exercise so you deserve more food."

I laughed myself out of that one and after a few weeks, I found those stats were right. My appetite decreased rather than increased. (I didn't say it dropped off completely. That'll be the day.)

Another plus for exercise is that it increases your energy. If you're feeling all dragged out after a hard day of hitting the books, take a brisk walk. Try it. You'll come back energized and eager to do something other than plop in front of the boob tube with a bag of potato chips.

Nothing to excess

Don't decide to run five miles twice a day, when the only exercise you've had for years is when the phys. ed. teacher forces you to run the track.

You can always increase the amount later when exercise has become a habit. Start with an extreme, unrealistic schedule and you set yourself up for failure. It's the same as deciding your weight goal. Select a regime you can live with.

Choose an exercise because you enjoy it, not because it's the "in" exercise of the moment. Some excellent ones are walking, jogging, cycling, swimming (really swimming, not paddling around), jumping rope and running in place. The last two are good because they leave you no excuse when it's raining or snowing or too hot or too cold or . . . .

But whichever you choose, make it as pleasant as possible. For instance, if you're running in place or jumping rope, do it to music or in front of the television.

If you're running in the park, try being Rocky and sing "Getting Stronger." Or slice the air with an occasional karate chop and sing out, "You're the best, nothing's ever gonna bring you down." Listen, a little bit of craziness can keep you from going insane.

All of the exercises mentioned above are aerobic exercises, meaning they get your heart beating fast. They're good for the heart and they burn lots of calories, but you need other kinds of exercise for firming up.

And there's more than one way . . .

First, I ought to mention such old standbys as sit-ups and leg raises. All right, I've mentioned them, but since I don't do them, I don't have anything to tell you about them. If you enjoy them—I don't recall ever meeting anyone who does—but if you do, go ahead. Ask your phys. ed. instructor for exercises that will firm up your special problem areas.

Me, I like isometrics. Great for the stomach and hips. All you need to do (and you can do this anyplace, anytime) is pull in your stomach as hard as you can, at the same time tucking in the buttocks as tightly as possible. Now, hold everything to

It's called exercise . . .

the count of ten. Relax. Repeat. Do this ten or twenty times throughout the day, the more the better, and I guarantee you'll see the difference. Isometrics don't burn many calories, and they certainly don't replace aerobic exercise, but they sure tighten up sagging muscles.

Look for ways to increase physical activity. If you drive, park farther from your destination and walk. If you take the bus, get off two stops before your regular stop. Take the stairs instead of the elevator. Don't sit if you can stand. Don't just stand there if you can move around. You'll see. It all helps.

Watch out for the rainmaker

Don't waste your money on exercise gimmicks. Don't be suckered by wild claims about such things as exercise belts worn around the waist that supposedly melt the fat away. There ain't no easy run, remember?

Even as I write, there's a fad going around called "passive exercise." Passive exercise is an electronic system. All you do is stand there (if you're either foolish or desperate enough) and they attach electrodes to your body. Then they zap you with electric current, which supposedly makes the muscles contract as they would if you were physically exercising. The trouble with most things like this is that more than your money is at stake. Most doctors say such an electronic exerciser can be dangerous for many people.

Let me remind you that people who get swindled are the ones who are trying to get something for nothing. What better pickings for the con artist than fat people who are forever searching for a painless way to get thin?

Just the other day I stumbled over my "twister," which had promised to get my waist measurement down to Scarlett O'Hara's size. I remember I used it twice.

43

13

Should I join
a diet club?

Diet clubs are everywhere. Weight Watchers, TOPS (Take Off Pounds Sensibly) and Overeaters Anonymous are three of the best known.

I belonged to one of these clubs for several years. I saw a few people succeed and many fail. By now, you should understand that when I say succeed, I mean keeping the weight off, not just losing it.

Everyone lost, but only a tiny percentage kept it off. Still, that small success rate can't be ignored. It might be you.

Some women attended meetings faithfully for years and never reached their goal. They enjoyed the meetings. It became a social outing. Well, you have to admit, it's better than hanging out in a bar. And who could deny that one day they might hear something at one of those meetings that would turn them around.

Take Lucille. She lost eighty pounds quickly, regained it quickly, and then attended meeting after meeting for two years,

Should I join a diet club?

never losing another ounce. She did manage not to gain more weight during those two years and I believe the club helped her do that. And then one day she got it together.

Perhaps it was something said at a meeting or the inspiration of a successful loser, but whatever the reason, she decided to try something weird, like losing without starving. She began shedding a half-pound each week, some weeks only a quarter-pound. It took a while, but she not only lost it all, she kept it off. Lucille still fights the good fight every day just as we all must, but she's no longer on the deadly stuff-and-starve routine.

A plus for Lucille was that she set her goal at a reasonable number. So many joined the club who had weighed 260 pounds for twenty years or more and set their goal at 105, a weight that—even if by some miracle they achieved it could never be maintained. It's all right to dream the impossible dream, but come on guys, there's a real world out there.

I also remember Becky, a young teenager, who wanted to lose ten pounds because her boyfriend thought she should. She'd lose five pounds one week and gain it back the next. We can only lose weight when *we* want to lose it, not because our boyfriends or our mothers think we should.

The dropout rate was high. People joined with great enthusiasm, but when they discovered that club or no club, it still came down to eating less, the enthusiasm died quickly.

There's a danger of falling into destructive patterns in a diet club. I knew women who gorged all week and then fasted for two days before they weighed in, just so they could have their names announced as a "no-gain." Immediately after the meeting, they headed for the nearest restaurant and began the cycle over again.

One of the nicest things about a diet club is that the members understand your problem. You can tell them about the time you ate a gallon of ice cream and three bags of potato chips and nobody will laugh or even look surprised. Instead, many will nod sympathetically and top your story with one of their own. Nobody will be disgusted or critical because they all know what you're talking about.

Diet clubs take away the loneliness that goes with fighting the fat battle, especially if everyone in your family is thin except you. You'll no longer feel that you're the only person in the world with this problem.

To wrap it up, diet clubs, like most things, have their good and bad points. In the end, it's all going to depend on you, whether or not you join a club. Nobody can lose your weight for you.

14

Heavy hints

"It is easier to suppress the first desire than to satisfy all that follow it." Ben Franklin said that over two hundred years ago, and it's still true today—especially about food.

When you have an overwhelming urge for a gooey wedge of chocolate cake or any other calorie-loaded goodie (and can you remember the last time you yearned for lettuce?) don't think you can handle it by taking a taste. Once you've had a taste, the craving will triple.

One way to resist taking the first bite is to make a deal with yourself.

"If I still crave this ice cream or candy or whatever tomorrow, I'll have it."

By tomorrow, the satisfaction of conquering a desire for twenty-four hours usually takes away the urge for whatever demon was driving you crazy yesterday. I'm not saying that by the next day there won't be some other demon to take its place. But, in that case, you'll just start all over again, "If I still crave this, etc., etc." Nothing's easy, Babe.

Another way to avoid that first, fatal taste is to DO SOMETHING (See Chapter 16). Don't just sit there listening to whatever is screaming at you from the fridge.

I must go down to the Thrift Shop again

When you're dropping several sizes, unless you just won the sweepstakes, you can't afford to run out and buy a wardrobe for each new size. What you can do is pick up jeans and skirts that fit at the Thrift Shop.

It's important that you do this so you can see your progress. If you walk around in shapeless, sloppy clothes, you'll feel shapeless and sloppy. You'll also feel like you're not getting anywhere with your diet. So, as soon as you drop a size, head for the Thrift Shop.

Heavy hints

One thing you can do when you're craving goodies is plan the wardrobe you'll buy when you reach your final goal. DON'T buy it now believing that will help you stay on your diet.

I don't know what idiot first thought up the idea of buying a small-sized dress and hanging it in the closet as an incentive. All it does is put more pressure on you—too much pressure and you'll eat. And every time you open your closet and see that stupid dress, you'll feel like a failure. Buy it when you can wear it.

15

True or false?

This is a quiz to determine your FIQ (Food Intelligence Quotient). If you answer all the questions correctly, you win a sugarless mint. If you miss one, you don't win a sugarless mint.

1. Bread is a great diet food.

TRUE. An ordinary slice of bread has about 75 cals. Slap a tablespoon of butter on it and you've suddenly got 175—but put the blame where it belongs—not on the bread.

Bread goes to the head of the class because it makes you feel full and satisfied. You don't need a huge amount of filling between the slices either. For instance, you can take a slice of diet cheese, add lettuce, tomato, bean sprouts, a little mustard, and you have a hefty, tasty sandwich for a mere 200 cals.

After eating that sandwich (create your own filling), you'll not only be better off nutritionally, but you'll be ever so much more contented than if you drink a can of that awful 300-calorie stuff that's supposed to replace a meal. Plus, you have 100 cals left. You could have a glass of skim milk and a vanilla wafer. Or a Popsicle. Or two Oreos.

Caution: When you buy bread, check the nutrition infor-

True or false?

mation. Sugar and molasses can up the count to 140 calories—double that of a plain slice.

2. Hard butter or margarine has more calories than soft or room-temperature spreads.

TRUE. Kind of. Actually, they have the same number of calories, but when you try to spread hard butter or margarine, you end up with big chunks (plus holes in the bread). At room temperature, spreads go on smooth and easy. It takes less to cover the bread. The result: Fewer calories.

The best deal, though, is to buy soft diet margarine. It's delicious, and one teaspoon covers a slice of bread nicely but adds only about seventeen cals.

3. Cereal is a smart choice for breakfast.

TRUE. A bowl of cereal (measure it out, please, according to what the box says is a serving) with low-fat milk and fruit is a filling and healthy breakfast. Forget all that stuff about a good hot breakfast unless you're talking oatmeal. A breakfast of bacon and eggs and toast dripping butter is not only loaded with calories but also with cholesterol.

Maybe you think it's only middle-aged people who should worry about cholesterol. Wrong.

During the Vietnam War, doctors were horrified at the amount of arteriosclerosis (a fancy name for fat clogging up the pipes) they found when performing autopsies on eighteen year olds.

That doesn't mean you should never eat another egg, but most of the expert docs say limit them to about three a week. And listen, you don't have to drown them in butter. Soft-boil 'em, hard-boil 'em, poach 'em, throw 'em in a mixer and drink them Rocky-style, or try my favorite way, fried in a nonstick skillet. If you insist on the buttery taste, use a smidge of diet margarine.

4. When I go to a restaurant, if I don't eat all the butter

they bring me, I'll be dumped in a bowl of Jell-O and allowed to shake to death.

FALSE. We chubs all belong to the Clean Plate Club, and it's time we cancelled our memberships. Watch Fat Fannie and Trim Tillie butter a roll in a restaurant. F.F. uses every smidgeon of her spread (pardon the expression) and licks the knife, but T.T. barely makes a dent in hers.

You can learn to get by on less. Just because it's there doesn't mean you must finish it. Develop taste. Learn to taste the bread itself. Learn to savor such things as texture.

If you're treating yourself to pancakes, don't drown them in a tidal wave of syrup. Give the pancake a chance. You'll be surprised how good it tastes. I was.

5. The brain needs sugar in order to function properly.

TRUE. But don't head for the candy store. As long as you're eating starch and protein, the body makes its own sugar.

6. Honey is healthier than sugar.

FALSE. Honey tastes good, and I like it, and I use it, but it's just another form of sugar with the same number of cals per teaspoon. The myth about the health benefits of honey began because it contains just a smidge of minerals. It's such a tiny smidge you'd have to eat gallons and gallons of honey to benefit from them.

Honey can sometimes be a good substitute for sugar because it's so concentrated that you don't need as much to get the same sweetness.

7. If I leave the table still wanting more, I'll be starved until the next meal—a pitiful creature gnawing on old Popsicle sticks.

FALSE. Unless it's Thanksgiving when we all eat until we can't move, we chubs are always going to want more. But if you push away from the table (and one pushaway is equal to five thousand pushups) and wait ten minutes, you'll begin to

True or false?

feel full. Try it. Anybody can hang on for ten minutes. But leave the table, or you'll be taking a dab of this, a dab of that, and five dabs equals a pound of fat on each thigh.

8. It's a good idea to ask my best friend to help with my diet.

FALSE. It's a better idea not to tell your friends about your diet at all. Even the best of friends can unwittingly sabotage your diet.

For one thing, if your friends are fat, they'll resent losing their partner in crime—eating partner that is. And there's a good chance you'll make them feel guilty, and nobody likes to feel guilty.

The main reason not to tell your friends, or your enemies, is that the more you talk about something, the more you begin to feel you've already done it. DO IT. DON'T TALK ABOUT HOW YOU'RE GOING TO DO IT.

9. If I keep the weight off for three months, I can overeat once in a while without gaining.

TRUE. But the key words here are "once in a while." You might get away with it for a week or so because your body hates changes and will work hard to keep things as they are. That's why it's hard to get the weight off in the first place.

So, if you overeat, the body will increase its metabolism to burn up the excess calories. For a while. But before long, just like the elastic in an old pair of sweats that have been stretched beyond endurance one too many times, the body will give up the fight, and you'll gain.

10. Good habits, unlike bad ones, are easy to break.

FALSE. A habit is a habit is a habit and once formed, whether good or bad, it takes an effort to break it.

For example, if you get used to brushing your teeth every night before bedtime, you'll soon find it almost impossible to go to bed without brushing.

53

How to be a reasonably thin teenage girl

In the same way, if you decide to abstain from eating after 8:00 P.M., and you're used to eating throughout the evening, it'll be difficult for you in the beginning. But each evening you succeed in not eating, you reinforce the habit. The habit will grow stronger and stronger until finally you'll need to make a real effort to eat after 8:00 P.M., even though you may crave something. And don't we always?

11. When I eat lunch or dinner out, I can guarantee I'll keep to my diet by ordering the diet plate.

FALSE. The usual diet plate consists of a hamburger patty, which has approximately 250 cals, a couple of crackers, 35 cals, half a cup of cottage cheese at 120 and a canned peach half for 100 cals.

Well, you can add can'tcha? That's 505 calories. You could have a quarter pounder and a glass of skim milk for 500 cals.

My maintenance calorie allotment doesn't allow me 500 cals for lunch. If I get caught away from home at lunchtime, I usually order either a tuna or an egg salad sandwich dry (without extra mayo), and a glass of iced tea with sweetener.

It's a different story though if I've planned to lunch with friends. I skip my morning and afternoon snacks which gives me 200 more cals to play with, and sometimes I steal from my dinner calories, thus having my big meal of the day at lunch instead of dinner.

As usual, you'll have to come up with your own way of handling these situations, but do forget about the so-called diet plate.

12. Well, then the salad bar is my best bet.

FALSE. "I'll just have a salad" is a very funny line. Watch the people at the salad bar. Look at all the fatties, with smug, self-sacrificing expressions dripping off their faces, building a salad. And boy, can we build a salad!

54

True or false?

First, a lettuce leaf. Then a couple of tablespoons of bacon bits (needs a little flavoring, you know) at 24 cals a tablespoon; throw on a couple of forkfuls of cheddar (after all, you need protein) at about 200 cals; a few pickled beets at 75 per half-cup; oh, and the grated egg yolk adds another 40, plus the garbanzos for 46 more calories. Already we're up to 385 cals, and we haven't begun to pour on the blue cheese at 80 cals a tablespoon. I can pour four tablespoons, which will bring the grand total to 705 cals, using my left hand. And hey, we forgot the peas, mushrooms, carrots, green pepper and of course the saltines.

Now you and I know we can build a salad for much less than 700 cals, but not without concentrating on it. You can cut out a big chunk of calories by carrying low-cal dressing in your purse, or by using one of the house dressings very, very sparingly. But the main cut can be made by using a lot more lettuce and a lot less of the trimmings. Learn not to kid yourself.

13. You can tell if a food has lots of calories simply by looking at it.

TRUE. At least some of the time. Such thick and creamy foods as split pea soup, clam chowder and pudding are high in calories whereas thin, watery soups are low. Foods that are naturally crispy like lettuce, carrots, radishes and onions are low. Foods like potato chips and onion rings that have been made crispy by frying them in grease are high.

All in all, if it's oily or gooey or creamy, you can be sure it's high-calorie, but if it's crunchy and crispy or see-through, it's probably low-cal. Just remember you can take a crunchy and crispy, dip it in a thick and creamy, and you've turned low-cal into high-cal.

Although you and I will always prefer thick and creamy, we can learn to control amounts. And we can learn to appreciate crisp and crunchy in ways we never have. As a friend said on her way to losing sixty pounds, "I never knew a crunchy, juicy, red apple could taste so good because I'd never let myself get hungry enough to really savor one."

14. If I eat grapefruit three times a day, the acid will neutralize the other calories I eat, and I'll lose without bothering about counting calories and all that stuff.

FALSE. Grapefruit's an excellent food and a good source of Vitamin C, but it has no little Pac-Man hiding inside to gobble up calories. Like the man said, if it sounds too good to be true, it probably is.

15. Yogurt is a low-calorie food.

FALSE. At least not the yogurt you're talking about. An eight-ounce container of plain yogurt has about 120 calories. That's a calorie bargain and it would serve as a milk substitute.

But, come on, you're not talking plain yogurt. You're talking yogurt with fruit and sugar. You're talking 250 and sometimes 300 cals for an eight-ounce container. That's not a low-cal food. Plus, it'll push your sugar-craving button.

You can take the plain yogurt and add sweetener and fresh fruit as a way of having this treat for fewer calories.

16. If it's liquid, it doesn't count.

FALSE. A regular cola drink has 100 cals. A glass of punch has 120, a six-ounce grape juice 120 and so on down the list. Water doesn't have any calories. Down the hatch!

17. Toast has fewer calories than plain bread.

FALSE. Toasting only removes water. Water doesn't have calories. Remember?

18. Liver is rich in Vitamin A.

TRUE. Because the liver is where people and animals store Vitamin A. And I'll bet you didn't know that the amount of Vitamin A in your serving of liver depends on the age of the animal whence it came—the older the animal, the more

True or false?

Vitamin A has accumulated. AND a cow that has been permitted to feed on grass will have more Vitamin A in her milk than one fed on grain only.

You ought to know these things. Who knows when you'll be asked?

19. Milk is nature's most nearly perfect food.

TRUE. Most of the known essential nutrients are found in milk but it has more of some than others. Forget any ideas of starting a milk-only diet.

20. If I stick to my diet without messing up, I'll lose weight every week.

FALSE. Eventually, you'll hit a leveling-off period. The diet experts call this a plateau. You may weigh the same for as long as three weeks. This is not a fun time. But grit your teeth (at least you can't eat that way) and hold on. You'll finally begin to lose again, probably dropping several pounds at once.

If you have a lot of weight to lose, you may hit a couple of these miserable plateaus. It's simply your body's way of adjusting and stabilizing itself.

21. Skipping meals is one way to lose weight.

FALSE. If you skip breakfast and/or lunch, you'll make up for it at dinner, eating more than if you'd had three average meals.

Also, the research guys have discovered that eating only one big meal a day may increase fat production. You may actually add more fat than if you'd spread the same amount of food over three meals. AND, it's a proven fact that fat people eat *fewer* meals a day than thin people. Think about that.

22. Vegetables are more nutritious if they are eaten raw.

FALSE. Uncooked veggies are surrounded by a cellulose layer that's hard to digest. The vitamins and minerals are more accessible in their cooked state. This does not mean cooking them to mush—just until they're tender but still slightly crunchy.

23. Anorexia nervosa is a country in Southeast Asia.

FALSE. Anorexia nervosa is a sickness in which adolescent girls and young women starve themselves to death. No matter how emaciated they become, they still see themselves as fat. Doctors don't know what triggers it although there are many theories.

My own theory is that it results from the constant pressure in our society (television, movies, books) that insists you cannot be too thin. *You can be too thin.* This is another reason I urge you throughout this book to be realistic—not fanatical—about your weight.

24. As long as it's a "health food," it's low in calories.

FALSE. Carrot cake is not low in calories.

25. Only old people need to worry about fiber in their diet.

FALSE. Everyone needs fiber. Researchers find out more and more every day about the benefits of fiber. For instance, they know that high-fiber diets help keep cholesterol low, which helps prevent heart attacks. They've also found that in societies where people consistently eat a high-fiber diet diabetes is almost unheard of.

If that doesn't interest you, let me remind you that enough fiber will keep you from becoming constipated. "How embarrassing," you say. Maybe. But also uncomfortable and *very* prevalent among dieters. It's often just one more excuse to give up on losing weight.

To put more fiber in your diet, eat whole grain breads and cereals. Eat fruits and veggies (eat your potato skin and don't peel apples and pears and such). Bananas and celery are good sources. So are nuts, but watch it, they're also high in calories.

16

Ten things to do when you're starving and it's still two hours until dinner

1. Take a walk down a well-traveled street. There's nothing like hearing a bunch of guys yelling, "Hey, Big Mama," to remind you why you're going to keep ignoring that voice calling from the fridge.

2. Take a bath—a nice, warm, bubbly bath. Just make sure you stand in front of a full-length mirror, unclothed, before getting into the tub. Talk about your motivations!

3. Pamper yourself. Try a new color eyeshadow, experiment with hairstyles, or give yourself a pro manicure.

4. Meditate. Learn the technique of visualization. Imagine yourself in a place where you remember being totally relaxed and carefree, whether it was the beach, the mountains or a disco.

As an example of how this works, let's say it's the beach. Send your mind back there. Feel the sun on your body. Hear

the surf pounding. Picture the seagulls gliding gracefully over-
head. Concentrate until that remembered tranquility returns.

OR, visualize yourself thin in that bikini you've always
dreamed of wearing, strolling down the beach with all eyes on
you. New girl in town.

OR, think of french fries. See them turn into globs of
yellow, gooky fat. Feel it running down your chin in greasy
streams onto your new, silk blouse. Watch big chunks of fat
fighting their way through your system—not making it out—
getting stuck in your arteries instead. Yech.

5. Brush your teeth.

Ten things to do when you're starving . . .

6. Do some exercises. They'll not only help get rid of your hunger by releasing stored sugar into your blood, but they'll make you aware of your body and certain, ah, problems.

7. If you enjoy handicrafts, get out your needlepoint or your candle-making kit, anything to keep your mind off food.

8. Remind yourself that dinner is not *that* far away, and the chances of your dying of malnutrition before then are minimal.

9. Remember Reward Day is coming.

10. Shake your piggy bank and go buy yourself a present. It needn't be expensive—a pretty comb for your hair, ribbons, nail polish, nail stick-ons—something that makes you feel feminine.

17

Fifty ways to lose
your blubber

1. Buy a scale that weighs accurately. I like digital scales because what you see is what you get. You can't jump around, or lean from side to side and make the weight change.

2. Buy a good calorie-counting book that has a complete list of foods. One of the best is published by the United States Government. It's called *Nutritive Value of Foods* and is available for $4.50 from the Superintendent of Documents, U.S. Government Printing Office, Washington, D.C. 20402.

Appendices in this book contain some calorie information to get you started, but it's too limited for the long haul.

3. Learn to tell the difference between fatigue and hunger. Never, *ever* eat because you're tired. Take a nap.

4. Keep your Emergency Box filled with a variety of interesting foods. Don't put the same old, dull things in it. Use your imagination.

5. Try to enlist your family's cooperation. Ask them not to bring high-calorie junk foods into the house. If they'll cooperate, that's another point for you. If they won't? Oh well,

Fifty ways to lose your blubber

the stuff is everywhere and control may as well start at home. DON'T use that as an excuse. Excuses are everywhere and if you want one, they're easy to find. But if you want to lose weight, you'll quit looking for them.

6. Keep green, seedless grapes in the freezer. They're not only delicious frozen, but it takes longer to eat a frozen grape.

7. For a treat, slice strawberries and sprinkle with Equal. Pour buttermilk over all. Let set a few hours or overnight. Scrumptious strawberries and cream! It sounds gross if you don't like buttermilk, but trust me. If you like sour cream, you'll like this.

8. Always carry no-cal sweetener in your purse.

9. Think before you eat. Every peanut must be counted. Believe me, your body is keeping track whether you are or not.

10. Don't skip meals.

11. Don't stuff and starve—gorging one day and starving the next—because the first thing you know the gorge days will outnumber the starve days.

12. Stay away from diets that cut out entire food groups. They're unhealthy and they don't work.

13. Eat slowly—savor—appreciate.

14. Learn to think like a thin person. Thin people think of having a *piece* of pie, not the *whole* pie.

15. Don't buy tent clothes you can hide in unless you intend to stay fat and wear tents the rest of your life.

16. When you eat *anything*, sit at a table or under a tree, but sit. Don't grab a sandwich for lunch and eat it en route somewhere. You won't remember eating it, and you'll still be hungry.

17. If you drink coffee or tea, learn to drink it black. I used to use coffee creamers because they only have seventeen cals per level teaspoon. Trouble was I never used level. By the time I got through with that teaspoon, I'd added at least 40

cals to my coffee. If you drink several cups a day, that adds up fast.

18. *Do* check out diet food products. *Don't* think because it's labeled "light" or "natural" that it's low calorie.

19. *Do* get back on your diet at the very next meal, no matter how badly you mess up.

20. Keep a record of what you eat each day—so you learn about your body and come to understand what you can and cannot get away with.

21. Plan, as best you can, the night before what you'll eat the next day. It's best to make decisions about food when you're not hungry.

22. Be realistic about how much you should weigh. RE-MEMBER, you're not concerned with how much weight you can lose, but with how much you can keep off.

23. If you're offered amphetamines (uppers) with the glowing promise you'll lose weight without being hungry—say "No, thank you." You've got one problem—you don't need another one. Besides which, they don't work either.

24. Do have a planned reward once a week to prevent a lethal attack of self-pity.

25. Plan ahead. You may be just a "wild and crazy" gal, but the secret word in dieting is planning, not impulse. Plan what you're going to eat and when you're going to eat it. Plan what you're going to do when you're feeling blue. Plan what you're going to do when you're stricken with a munchies attack. Plan, plan, plan. Think of every possible situation and live it in your imagination in preparation for the real thing.

26. Hold the sauces, *not* the pickles and the lettuce. Learn to eat veggies plain. Learn that a sandwich can taste as good with a teaspoon of mayo as with a tablespoon.

27. Eat the whole piece of fruit rather than drinking the juice. It adds fiber to your diet and makes you feel full longer.

Fifty ways to lose your blubber

28. Don't buy presweetened cereal, because you'll be tempted to eat it out of the box for a snack.

29. Weigh only once a week until you reach your goal weight.

30. Don't become a diet bore, and make your diet your only topic of conversation.

31. Don't be conned into buying useless exercising gadgets that you'll use once or twice and toss in the closet.

32. Take advantage of the helpful diet foods—especially diet margarines and mayonnaise which have half the cals of regular (50 per tablespoon rather than 100) and they taste good. Try the low-sugar jellies and the low-cal cocoa mixes for a treat.

33. Don't jump into your sweats the minute you come home from school. They're too comfortable and give the illusion of thinness (as long as you don't look in a mirror). Wear something with a snug waist that keeps you aware of your problem.

34. Don't endow certain foods with magical qualities. It's amazing, for example, how many people think of cottage cheese when they think diet. They hate it, but there they are choking it down because they're on a diet. It's a perfectly good food, loaded with protein. But don't eat it because you're dieting. Eat it only if you enjoy it. I don't know where its low-cal reputation came from because it has approximately 130 cals per half-cup.

35. Don't use chewing gum for a pacifier. It activates the salivary glands and stimulates your appetite. Also, you're apt to pop in a fresh stick every ten minutes to get the sugar, and a single piece can have anywhere from 5 to 30 cals.

36. Don't do something idiotic like start smoking to keep your weight down. It won't work, and you'll have one more monkey on your back.

37. In the words of Thoreau, "Simplify, simplify." Learn to eat food plain without sauce and gravies. Veggies without butter.

38. Pass up the chips and dip and other appetizers. I don't know why they're called appetizers. I could use up a day's calorie allotment before I reached the dinner table, and that was with one hand in my pocket.

39. Trim every speck of fat from your meat.

40. Remove skin from poultry before eating.

41. Don't add salt to food at the table. Use it lightly when cooking. Salt holds onto water which holds onto fat and besides that, too much isn't good for you.

42. Remember that any food can be fattening if you eat enough of it. At the same time, any food can be low-calorie if the portion is small enough.

43. Learn the calorie count of foods you eat often, and learn your Basic 4 food groups.

44. Learn to say, "No, thank you," to food without explaining every hunger pang of your diet.

45. Don't lie to yourself. It's true that you may retain water just prior to your menstrual period, which may show up on the scale. But don't be like the lady in my diet club who used this excuse every week. One week she was up in weight because it was the week before her period, the next week she was up because it was the week of her period, and the next it was because it was the week after and once more around the track.

46. Learn to juggle foods. Mashed potatoes and corn are both starchy foods. You eat one or the other at a meal, not both.

47. Learn to carry conversation when you're sharing a meal. Don't concentrate only on stuffing food in your mouth.

48. Do get some kind of exercise. It not only burns calories and makes you feel better, but it makes you aware of your body.

Fifty ways to lose your blubber

49. Resign from the Clean Plate Club. Learn to stop eating when you're full—not when the plate's empty.

50. Lay a small guilt trip on yourself. Look around you at the handicapped people who can do nothing but live with their disabilities the best way they can. You don't have to live with yours. You have a choice.

And if you think overweight is not a handicap, look around again. The painful misshapen feet stuffed into and overlapping the shoes, the wheezing and panting after only mild exertion—even talking, the pasty complexions, the high blood pressure, the stroke waiting just outside the door, and the diabetes lurking in the wings.

Look, and make your choice, and thank God you have a choice.

18

Let's talk
maintenance

Do you want to be fat and on a diet the rest of your life? That may sound like a contradiction, but think about it.

Don't you know people who've been on a diet for years, and they're still fat—in most cases fatter. They go from one fad diet to another, losing a few pounds and gaining back a few pounds extra.

The sad thing is that they never really enjoy eating either, because they're always feeling guilty for going off their diet.

Since you're going to break this dumb pattern, I want to talk a little about what to do when you reach your chosen weight.

First, you continue doing most of the things you've been doing on your reducing diet. That puts you far ahead of the majority of dieters already.

YOU know how to plan what you're going to eat, and YOU know how to count past 1,000. Most women go on 1,000-cal diets and they never learn to count higher than that. That's one reason most of them regain their weight.

Let's talk maintenance

Let's say you've reached your goal of 125 pounds. To maintain that weight, you must count to 1,875. If you don't count, you'll be eating 2,000 cals before you know it and by the time you know it, you'll be in trouble. YOU ARE NEVER GOING TO STOP COUNTING.

When you first reach goal, proceed very, very carefully, adding calories slowly until you reach your maintenance allowance. Don't stop dieting one day and go to total maintenance calories the next. Sneak up on it. Give your body and your mind time to adjust. Add about 75 cals a day until you reach your limit.

Once you've held your goal weight for three months (that's in a row, guys), your body is accustomed to that weight and will try hard to keep it there.

After this three-month adjustment period, you can experiment with your maintenance program a bit. Don't get extreme. But if you want to splurge on a hot fudge sundae, or if a family reunion dinner is coming up, you can count your maintenance calories over a three-day period.

If you weigh 125 pounds, you need 1,875 cals a day, OR 5,625 over a period of three days to maintain that weight. If you eat 3,500 cals on the big day, that leaves 2,125 for the next two days, or 1,062 per day. By spreading the calories over three days, you won't end up with a starving day. Starving, as we all know, leads to binges.

You can do this one of two ways. If the reunion is on Saturday, you can either plan your 1,062-cal days for the Thursday and Friday before OR for the Sunday and Monday following. Try it both ways and go with the one that works best.

In an ideal world, we'd go to the big bash, eat moderately and not mess up our weight at all. But we're talking reality here. (You know Aunt Bessie will bring her banana split cake!) So . . . PLAN, PLAN, PLAN.

How to be a reasonably thin teenage girl

For the rest of your life . . .

Reaching your weight goal is a heady victory, but it's only the first round of a fight that will go on the rest of your life. That's not as depressing as it sounds. It's not that you're going to walk around with clenched teeth and fists twenty-four hours a day fighting off Twinkies.

Oh, there'll be those kind of days. Don't start kidding yourself at this point. I recently read about a woman who had one of those bizarre operations closing off part of her stomach, after which she lost something like 150 pounds. Later she began to regain the weight because although she could only hold three or four ounces of food at a meal, she figured out that she could sneak in another four ounces in between meals. Who was the woman fooling?

The main reason losers regain their weight is that most of them have been living on three hard-boiled eggs and a lettuce leaf a day. So, of course, they go crazy when they get a taste of something they enjoy. Isn't it lucky that YOU haven't been eating like that?

Another reason is that too many chubs think of a diet as something that lasts only for a certain period of time. "Thank goodness, that's over," they say with a sigh, and immediately return to their old way of eating. But YOU have understood all along that the important thing is not reaching your goal, but being able to stay there.

Now all YOU need do is continue the good habits you've learned: juggle your foods, count your calories, cover the Basic 4, plan ahead and keep moving.

The only change you'll make will be in your weighing habits. Dr. Theodore Van Itallie, director of obesity research,

Let's talk maintenance

St. Lukes Hospital in New York City says, "The price of leanness, like liberty, is eternal vigilance." Which, according to my translation, means: you will weigh every morning for the rest of your life. When the scale moves up two pounds, you will cut back until the scale moves back down two pounds. GET IT WHILE IT'S STILL TWO POUNDS. Two pounds is so much easier to lose than ten, fifteen, and so on. And we know how easy it is to reach "so on."

A brief warning here. Don't turn into one of those people who forget they were ever fat and lose all compassion for people who still are. It's easier to be humble if you remember you're just a few cream puffs away from being back where you were.

19

Happy
trails . . .

Now, it's up to you. You can do it, you know. You can do anything you set your mind to. And success has an interesting side effect: more success. You manage to do one impossible thing and you find yourself saying, "Hey, if I could do THAT, I can certainly do THIS."

Once you succeed in reaching your goal weight, you'll notice other problems in your life start to fall in line. That's not because being thinner solves all problems, it's because success in one area breeds success in another. And so on down the chain.

I tried to write this book with humor because if we can't laugh at ourselves, we're really in trouble. But underneath the funny stuff, I've been dead serious because I know there's nothing humorous about being fat and feeling ugly. I know because I've been there. I'm not there anymore and you don't have to be either.

Send me a picture of the new you.

Comparing Fat Fannie and Trim Tillie

Fat Fannie and Trim Tillie have a lot in common. They're both in tenth grade, they're both fifteen, they're both blondes and they're both 5'3" tall. There is, however, one BIG difference. Fat Fannie weighs 150 and Trim Tillie weighs 115. Why do you suppose that is? Let's look at a typical eating day.

FAT FANNIE'S MENU BREAKFAST	TRIM TILLIE'S MENU BREAKFAST	
F.F. NEVER eats breakfast	6 oz. orange juice	84
	Cereal with sweetener,	
	1 serving	110
	8 oz. low-fat milk,	
	(use half on cereal)	140
		334

MID-MORNING SNACK	MIDMORNING SNACK	
F.F. NEVER eats before lunch, but since it's only liquid, she will have	1 large apple	100
1 12-oz. cola 145		

Appendix A

LUNCH		LUNCH	
Big Mac	550	Quarter Pounder	420
French Fries	180	Diet cola	0
1 12-oz. cola	145		——
	——		420
	875		

MID-AFTERNOON SNACK		MID-AFTERNOON SNACK	
1 Snickers bar	130	1 Jell-O Pudding Pop	90

DINNER		DINNER	
1 serving green salad with 2 tbs. regular French dressing	150	1 serving green salad with 2 tbs. low-calorie French dressing	100
2 cups of beef stew	420	2 cups of beef stew	420
1 slice of bread with 1 tbs. butter	175	1 breadstick	40
8-oz. whole milk	160	8-oz. nonfat milk	80
	——		——
	905		640

EVENING SNACK		EVENING SNACK	
1½ cups candy-coated popcorn	220	4 cups plain popcorn, popped without oil	100

TOTAL FOR THE DAY	2,275*	TOTAL FOR THE DAY	1,684*

*170 more calories than the 2250 needed to maintain her present weight.

*41 calories less than the 1725 needed to maintain her present weight.

How to be a reasonably thin teenage girl

You can see that on this "typical day," both girls stayed close to the number of cals needed to maintain their weights. Now you and I know that typical days don't come around very often. Tillie will have higher-calorie days, but because she's learned to juggle, she'll compensate with lower-calorie days to keep her weight stable. Fannie, I'm afraid, will have only higher-calorie days if she keeps following the same eating pattern.

The biggest difference in their eating habits is the choices they make. When T.T. has a cola drink, it's the sugarless kind. F.F., on the contrary, used 435 calories on Cokes alone! Choosing a Big Mac over a Quarter Pounder cost her 130 cals, regular salad dressing over diet, 50, whole milk over nonfat, 80 and candy-coated popcorn over plain, 120. Put that in your calculator! You'll find it adds up to 815 unnecessary calories. That's without even mentioning the pathetic choice of snacks. And remember that all those sweets push Fannie's sugar button, causing her to feel hungry all the time.

If you check the chart in Chapter 5, you'll see that F.F., at her present weight, can eat the same amount of calories as T.T. and LOSE a pound a week.

Fannie must learn to think before she eats. Fannie must accept the fact that she's not going to get thin in a week. Fannie must stop going on those hopeless crash diets every other month, during which she loses five pounds and gains back eight.

O.K. Maybe Fat Fannie never will be as thin as Trim Tillie. Maybe she can only maintain a 130-or-125-pound weight. But think how much trimmer she'll look at that weight. Think how much better she'll like herself. Think how nobody will EVER call her Fat Fannie again. Go for it, Fannie.

Big four calorie chart

In each of the four groups, the amount listed is considered a serving. For the most part, the calories are estimated (within a high-low range). If you want to be more exact, buy a complete calorie counter book (see Chapter 17).

One more thing. And isn't there always? Remember who you're cheating if you fudge (sorry) on counting calories. A 2-ounce, lean, broiled hamburger is just that. If you add a bun, that's 150 more cals. If you splash on a tablespoon of catsup, that's 15 more. Throw a tablespoon of butter on half a cup of cauliflower and instead of 24 cals, you've suddenly got 125. Don't con yourself.

Meat, poultry, fish and beans group

(Provides protein, iron, thiamin, riboflavin, niacin and vitamin B_{12}.)
You need TWO servings a day from this group. Each serving contains from 125–150 calories.

Beans, baked	½ cup
Chicken, baked or broiled, skin removed	3 oz.
Eggs, boiled, poached or fried in non-stick skillet	2
Fish, broiled	3 oz.
Ham, fat trimmed	3 oz.

Hamburger, lean, broiled	2 oz.
Hot dog	1
Lamb, fat trimmed	3 oz.
Liver, calf, broiled	2 oz.
Pork chops, fat trimmed	2 oz.
Steak, sirloin, fat trimmed	2 oz.
Tuna, water-packed	4 oz.
Turkey, white meat	3 oz.

Mixed-up stuff in this group

	Serving	Calories
Beef stew, homemade with lean beef	1 cup	210
(Counts for 1 meat and 1 vegetable)		
Chili with beans	½ cup	170
Lasagne	4 oz.	200
(Counts for 1 meat and 1 bread)		
Macaroni and cheese	¾ cup	260
(Counts for 1 meat and 1 bread)		
Meat loaf	3 oz.	170
Spaghetti with tomato sauce and cheese	1 cup	260
(Counts for 1 meat and 1 bread)		

Milk and cheese

(Provides protein, calcium, phosphorus, vitamins A, D and riboflavin)

Appendix B

You need THREE servings a day from this group. Each serving contains from 80–100 calories.

Buttermilk	1 cup
Cheddar cheese	1 oz.
Cottage cheese	½ cup
Low-fat milk	¾ cup
Nonfat milk	1 cup
Yogurt, plain	¾ cup

Vegetable and fruit

(Provides vitamins A and C, fiber and folic acid)

You need FOUR servings a day from this group. HOW-EVER, all veggies are not created equal, so we'll divide them into two groups.

VEGGIE GROUP #1

One half-cup, PLAIN, equals one serving and has 25 cals.

Asparagus	*Cauliflower*	*Onions*
Bean sprouts	*Celery*	*Radishes*
Beets (not pickled)	*Cucumbers*	*Sauerkraut*
Broccoli	*Green pepper*	*String beans*
Brussels sprouts	*Lettuce*	*Tomatoes*
Cabbage	*Mushrooms*	*Tomato juice*
		Zucchini squash

VEGGIE GROUP #2 — STARCHY VEGGIES

Each serving, PLAIN, has 70–100 calories each.

Corn	⅓ cup
Corn on cob	1 small
Peas	½ cup
Potato, baked	1 small
Potato, mashed	½ cup
Potatoes, french fried	8 pieces
Potato chips	15 chips
Sweet potato	¼ cup

Fruits and fruit juice

(40–50 cals per serving)

Apple	1 small
Apple juice or cider	⅓ cup
Apricots	2 medium
Banana	½ small
Cantaloupe	¼ small
Cherries	10 large
Grapefruit	½
Grapefruit juice	½ cup
Grapes	12
Grape juice	¼ cup
Nectarine	1 small
Orange	1 small
Orange juice	⅓ cup
Peach	1 medium
Pear	1 small

Appendix B

Pineapple	½ cup
Pineapple juice	½ cup
Plums	2 medium
Raisins	2 tbs.
Strawberries	¾ cup
Tangerine	1 medium
Watermelon	1 cup

Bread and cereal

(Provides B vitamins, iron, protein and fiber)

You need FOUR servings a day from this group. Each serving contains 75–100 cals.

Bagel	½ small
Biscuit	1 small
Boston brown bread	½ inch slice
Bran muffin	1 small
Bun, hamburger or hot dog	½
Cereal, dry (not granola-type)	¾ cup
Cereal, cooked	¾ cup
Cracker, graham	2
Cracker, saltine	6
English muffin	½ small
Pasta, plain	½ cup
Popcorn, plain	4 cups
Pretzels (1 ring)	10
Rice	½ cup
Tortilla	1

Fun snacks that won't break the calorie bank

SNACK	TOTAL CALS
1 medium orange	
2 Saltines	100
1 Jell-O Pudding Pop	90
1 Dole's Frozen Juice Bar	70
1 cup fresh strawberries, plain	
2 graham crackers	100
½ Cantaloupe	
2 Vanilla wafers	100
6-oz. can grapefruit juice	
20 thin pretzel sticks	100
Popsicle, all fruit flavors	70
6 Animal crackers	
4-oz. nonfat milk	112
1 slice bread with 2 tsp. low-sugar jelly	
8-oz. glass Crystal Light Punch	100
½ oz. pkg. raisins	80

Fun snacks . . .

6-oz. V-8 juice	
11 Cheez-Its	100
Baked apple—baked in diet black cherry cola	100
½ oz. pkg. Skinny Haven Munchies	
4 oz. apple juice	120
1 Guidd's Ice Juice	58
4 cups popcorn, popped without oil	100
Dreamsicle	70
1 slice diet cheese plus 2 saltines	
1 diet cola	100
1 cup diet Ovaltine	
1 small oatmeal cookie	100

Index

84

Index